ALLEN COUNTY PUBLIC LIBRARY

3 1833 01571 1812

P9-EEI-737

jB M272a
Asimov, Isaac
Ferdinand Magellan

DO NOT REMOVE
CARDS FROM POCKET

3/92

ALLEN COUNTY PUBLIC LIBRARY

FORT WAYNE, INDIANA 46802

You may return this book to any agency, branch,
or bookmobile of the Allen County Public Library.

DEMCO

ISAAC ASIMOV'S
Pioneers of Science and Exploration

FERDINAND MAGELLAN

Opening the Door to World Exploration

by Isaac Asimov

Gareth Stevens Children's Books
MILWAUKEE

Allen County Public Library
Ft. Wayne, Indiana

For a free color catalog describing Gareth Stevens' list of high-quality children's books, call 1-800-341-3569 (USA) or 1-800-461-9120 (Canada).

Picture Credits
The Bettmann Archive 21; Gareth Stevens, Inc. 6-7; Giraudon/Art Resource 12; Mary Evans Picture Library 7 (both), 18, 19, 27, 32; Mark Mille 34-35 (map); William L. Clements Library 8.

Library of Congress Cataloging-in-Publication Data

Asimov, Isaac, 1920-
    Ferdinand Magellan : opening the door to world exploration / by Isaac Asimov.
      p. cm. — (Isaac Asimov's pioneers of science and exploration)
    Includes bibliographical references and index.
    Summary: Presents the story of the Portuguese explorer who became the first European to cross the Pacific Ocean and whose expedition completed its voyage around the world after his death en route.
    ISBN 0-8368-0560-7
    1. Magalhães, Fernão de, d. 1521—Journeys—Juvenile literature. 2. Explorers—Portugal—Biography—Juvenile literature. 3. Voyages around the world—Juvenile literature. [1. Magellan, Ferdinand, d. 1521. 2. Explorers. 3. Voyages around the world.] I. Title. II. Series: Asimov, Isaac, 1920- Isaac Asimov's pioneers of science and exploration.
G420.M2A85   1991
910'.92—dc20   91-9207

A Gareth Stevens Children's Books edition

Edited, designed, and produced by
Gareth Stevens Children's Books
1555 North RiverCenter Drive, Suite 201
Milwaukee, Wisconsin 53212, USA

Text copyright © 1991 by Nightfall, Inc. and Martin H. Greenberg. End matter copyright © 1991 by Gareth Stevens, Inc. Format copyright © 1991 by Gareth Stevens, Inc. First published in the United States and Canada by Gareth Stevens, Inc. All rights reserved. No part of this book may be reproduced or used in any form or by any means without permission in writing from Gareth Stevens, Inc.

Editors: Amy Bauman, Barbara Behm
Editorial assistants: Scott Enk, Diane Laska, Jamie Daniel
Designer: Kristi Ludwig
Picture researcher: Daniel Helminak
Assistant picture researcher: Diane Laska
Illustrator: J. Rick Karpinski

Printed in the United States of America

1 2 3 4 5 6 7 8 9 95 94 93 92 91

CONTENTS

THE MAGNIFICENT PACIFIC

The last of the four ships moved through the twisting channel of water. All around, a storm raged. For months, the fleet's captain and crews had sailed along the coast of South America, searching for a water passageway, called a strait, that would connect the Atlantic Ocean with the Pacific Ocean.

Finally, they came to water leading inward between two landmasses — the southern part of mainland South America and Tierra del Fuego. This might be the strait that would lead them all the way through to the other side. They couldn't be sure until they traveled it. If they were wrong, they would have to turn around and sail back out again. Furthermore, the men were becoming mutinous because of the miserable conditions. Only the iron will of the captain — Ferdinand Magellan — kept the voyage going.

For five weeks, the ships sailed through the stormy channel. Then one day, the violent storms were gone. The channel suddenly opened before them, revealing a vast, peaceful ocean. Magellan joyfully fell to his knees. He named the water before him the Pacific Ocean because it was so pacific, or peaceful. Little did he know that the hardest part of the voyage was still ahead. The Pacific Ocean was to prove not so peaceful after all.

1

A WORLD FOR THE EXPLORING

Captain Ferdinand Magellan, who made this historic voyage and named the Pacific Ocean, was born in 1480 in Portugal, a coastal nation in southwestern Europe. In Portuguese, his native language, his name was Fernão de Magalhães.

The country of Portugal had always hungered for the silks and spices of the Far East. These valuable treasures were brought to Europe by slow and expensive land routes. In 1425, it

In 1425, Prince Henry (opposite, left) suggested that sailing to the Far East might be a quicker route than traveling by land. In 1497, Vasco da Gama (opposite, right) navigated such a route by sailing around the southern tip of Africa. These men, seen against a backdrop of the Cape of Good Hope at Africa's southern tip, contributed much to Portugal's ranking as a powerful sea empire.

occurred to a Portuguese prince, known as Henry the Navigator, that a more direct route to the Far East might be found by sailing around southern Africa.

For the next sixty years, Portuguese explorers inched their ships down the coast of Africa. Finally, in 1487, a Portuguese navigator, Bartholomew Dias, reached the southern tip of Africa. But it was not until ten years later that another Portuguese navigator, Vasco da Gama, would finally sail around Africa and reach India.

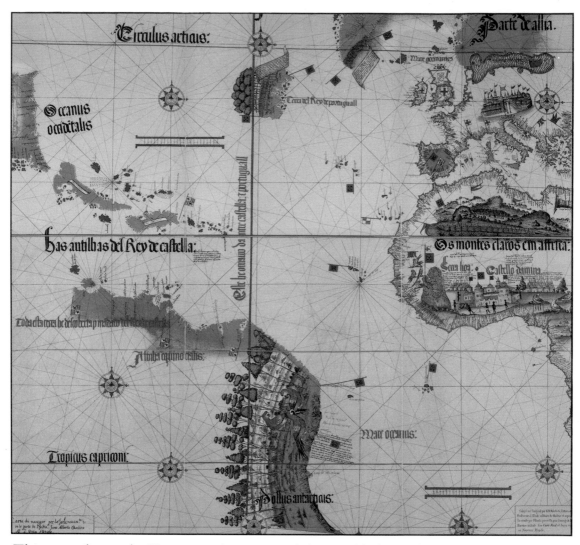

This map shows the Europeans' concept of the world about the time of Magellan's explorations. Both Spain and Portugal were hungrily exploring and claiming new lands at this time, and to settle any disputes, Pope Alexander VI drew a line (shown here at the map's center) dividing the new lands between the two countries.

Throughout the 1400s, both Spain and Portugal were eagerly exploring the world. Brave sailors navigated the seas and claimed many new lands for their countries. To avoid any disputes, Pope Alexander VI divided the new lands between these two powerful countries. In 1493, he drew a line down the middle of a map of the Atlantic Ocean. He ordered that non-Christian lands east of the line belong to Portugal. Non-Christian lands west of

8

the line would go to Spain. This order would one day change Magellan's life.

Ferdinand Magellan was born in 1480, the son of Portuguese nobility. When he was thirteen, he was sent to court to learn the ways of the people of his social class.

Ferdinand became a page to King John II and Queen Leonor of Portugal. At court, Ferdinand and the other pages studied subjects such as music and dancing. But because King John was fascinated by the sea, the boys were also given lessons in geography and navigation.

When Ferdinand arrived at court, Christopher Columbus was just returning to Spain from his voyage to the New

By the end of the fifteenth century, sailors' stories of sea exploration had captured the imagination of all Portugal.

World. This was probably Ferdinand's first exposure to the excitement of ocean travel and voyages to new lands. Upon hearing the stories of Columbus's journey, Ferdinand fell in love with the sea.

Things changed for the boys at court when King John was murdered. John's brother-in-law, Duke Manuel, then became king, and he had no interest in sea exploration. This was a difficult time for Ferdinand, who dreamed of becoming a sailor and an explorer. For six years, he begged the king to allow him to leave the court to follow this dream. For six years, the king ignored the young man.

But Ferdinand's luck would change when Vasco da Gama returned to Portugal from India in 1499. Da Gama's ships were loaded with the riches that the Portuguese had been dreaming of for years. It was then that King Manuel realized what could be gained from sea exploration. Such exploration, for instance, could increase Portugal's role in the trade of silks and spices. Spices were especially important products at this time because people had learned to use them to preserve food. The riches that could be made in the trading of spices was another reason to explore. The king knew that Arab traders were growing wealthy by bringing spices from the East to Europe by way of the Arabian Sea and Africa.

Again Ferdinand asked for permission to become a sailor. Now the time was right. The king had changed his feelings about the sea. This time he let Ferdinand go.

Opposite: For years, Ferdinand Magellan begged King Manuel to allow him to leave his duties at court and go to sea. Some historians suggest that the king did not like Magellan.

2

A LIFE AT SEA

At twenty-five years of age, Magellan decided to devote his life to the sea. Thoughts of trade had lured him to this decision. He knew an increase in trade could make Portugal a prosperous country. Beyond this, Magellan was deeply religious, and he longed to spread his Christian beliefs to others. But most of all, the fearless young man thirsted for adventure.

Until this time, Portugal had sailed its ships mainly along the coasts of the Mediterranean Sea and northwest Africa. In these regions, the Portuguese sailors had taken over seaports and

Above and opposite: By the 1500s, Lisbon, the capital of Portugal, had become a bustling seaport. It was here, while serving as a page in the royal court of King John II and Queen Leonor, that Ferdinand Magellan first dreamed of going to sea.

set up trading stations, conquering many of the native people that they encountered. Because the Portuguese had cannons and gunpowder, this was an easy task.

By the early 1500s, then, Portugal had become a powerful sea-trading empire. Its only competition was Spain. And Spain was no longer allowed to explore territory that lay east of the pope's dividing line.

The success of da Gama's voyage filled King Manuel with thoughts of power and riches. In 1504, he sent a fleet of twenty-two fighting ships to the Far East under the

command of Francisco de Almeida. Almeida's orders were to explore and trade but also, more important, to conquer. His fleet was to chase the Arab traders from the African coast and establish its own bases on the Indian coast. Until that time, the Arabs had controlled trade on the Indian Ocean.

With the king's approval, Magellan enlisted on one of the ships bound for the Far East. At long last, he was headed out to sea.

The Portuguese sailors fought two battles with the Arabs and won both. By 1509, the Portuguese had added the Indian Ocean to their domain. The real prize, however, was the Indonesian islands, which were rich in spices. The Portuguese pushed eastward until they reached Malacca, on the Malay Peninsula. This important port controlled the strait leading to the islands.

The sultan of Malacca must have heard that the Portuguese had defeated the Arabs. To protect his

On his first sea voyage, Magellan served under Francisco de Almeida. He was one of 1,980 men aboard twenty-two ships that sailed to the Far East with orders to explore, trade . . . and conquer.

lands from the invaders, he pretended to be friendly, offering to trade peacefully with them. Secretly, however, he planned to attack them.

From the start, Magellan was suspicious of the sultan. When the attack came, he and the other Portuguese sailors fought fiercely. Although they lost a ship and sixty men, they defeated the Malaccans. It was probably then that Magellan's bravery earned him a promotion to ship's officer.

The Portuguese ships went on to explore the other Indonesian islands to complete the Portuguese trading empire.

By 1512, Magellan was back in Lisbon, the capital of Portugal. He was a captain now. He had proven himself in battle and had also stopped a mutiny on the Portuguese ships. In the process, he had been wounded twice.

Magellan had done enough to deserve a rest, but he didn't want one. Portugal was fighting Morocco, across the narrow Strait of Gibraltar off North Africa, so he hurried to join the battle. Again he took part in a victory, and again he was wounded. This time it was his knee, and it was so bad that he would walk with a limp for the rest of his life.

After the battle, Magellan was put in charge of the cattle and horses captured from the Moroccans. Word spread that he had sold the livestock and made a huge profit for himself. A proud man, Magellan did not defend himself against these rumors. Perhaps he thought that his honesty and loyalty were so well known that he needed no defense.

When he returned to Lisbon in November 1514, Magellan asked for an increase in his pension because his injuries had disabled him. But King Manuel had heard the stories about Magellan selling the livestock. The king believed the stories and refused Magellan's request.

In 1516, Magellan again asked for an increase and was again refused. In fact, King Manuel discharged Magellan. Furious, Magellan swore he'd get revenge on King Manuel and the country that had betrayed him.

Opposite: When Magellan returned to Portugal following his time in the East, he found he had lost favor with King Manuel. In 1516, the king publicly dismissed Magellan from his service. The shame Magellan felt because of the king's treatment caused the explorer to turn his back on his homeland.

3

ANOTHER ROUTE TO FORTUNE

Through the late 1400s and early 1500s, European knowledge of the world expanded rapidly with each new expedition to the New World. Explorers such as Amerigo Vespucci, from Italy, contributed much to the settlement of the new lands.

In 1502, an Italian navigator named Amerigo Vespucci said that what Columbus had actually happened upon was a "new world." Vespucci also said that beyond the new world was a second ocean. Beyond this second ocean, he concluded, Asia could be found. Vespucci was correct. That is why the new lands were eventually called the Americas in his honor, rather than being named for Columbus.

A few years later, in 1513, a Spanish explorer, Vasco Núñez de Balboa, entered the Isthmus of Panama. Balboa didn't know that Panama was just a narrow strip of land. He explored inland from the shores of the Atlantic Ocean, searching for gold. He didn't find any, but after a few miles of travel, he came to what looked like another ocean. He called it the South Sea because the Atlantic Ocean was to the north of Panama and this new body of water was to the south.

For more than twenty years, Europe had been haunted by the dream of reaching the Far East by sailing to the west. Columbus was sure he had reached Asia when he crossed the Atlantic in 1492, but not everyone agreed. After all, the coastal lands he explored showed no signs of the great civilizations of China or India.

The Spanish conquistador and explorer Vasco Núñez de Balboa was another whose work influenced many people after him. In 1513, while exploring the Isthmus of Panama, Balboa came upon the Pacific Ocean. He was the first European to see the ocean from its eastern edge.

Ferdinand Magellan had heard of Vespucci's theory and of Balboa's discovery. He was convinced that Balboa had discovered the second ocean and that beyond that second ocean was Asia.

Magellan had also figured out something else. When Pope Alexander VI had drawn his line on a map of the Atlantic Ocean to separate the lands belonging to Spain and Portugal, he had not continued the line around to the other side of the globe.

Magellan believed that if Spanish ships could sail far enough westward, they could reach the Far East without crossing the pope's line. They could then freely trade with the Far Eastern lands in a completely legal way. If Magellan could convince the Spaniards of this and establish them in the Far East, he would have his revenge on Portugal and King Manuel.

But Magellan knew there was one catch to his plan — North and South America. No one knew for certain that a ship could travel through these huge landmasses and reach the second ocean. But there were rumors that a strait existed. Magellan intended to find it.

Magellan then began trying to convince the Spaniards that a strait could be found. To the Spaniards, Magellan was not an impressive figure. He was short, and his injuries had left him with a limp. But they knew of his great war record and of his bravery.

Some of the Spanish nobles were also impressed by the fact that Portugal had turned Magellan down and that he was now coming before Spain. After all, Portugal had also turned down Columbus, who had gone on to become so successful for Spain. Then, too, Magellan fell in love with the daughter of a prominent Spanish official. That softened Spanish opinion about him even more.

Only the king could supply Magellan with the ships and the men he would need for the voyage. Finally, Magellan was introduced to King Charles I, Spain's new king. Charles was a young, enthusiastic king. He had been looking for a way to increase Spain's empire. One by one, Charles's trusted advisers came to him, urging him to take a chance on the great adventurer Magellan.

Below: Ships are loaded with supplies in preparation for Magellan's journey.

Above: Charles I, king of Spain, did eventually agree to sponsor Magellan's quest for the second ocean.

This, they said, could be Spain's big chance.

The Portuguese even helped Magellan's project. When they found out about it, they did their best to stop it. This made Spain even more eager to pursue the expedition.

So in 1518, about six months after Magellan first came to Spain, King Charles agreed to send him on a quest for the second ocean. He assigned Magellan five ships and about 270 men. He also promised the explorer a share in any profits that the voyage might bring.

A VOYAGE INTO HISTORY

On September 20, 1519, five ships — the *San Antonio*, the *Trinidad*, the *Concepción*, the *Victoria*, and the *Santiago* — set sail on what was to be one of the greatest sea voyages ever made.

Life on board the ships was difficult for the sailors. The ships were cramped, crowded, and infested with rats and lice. Worse yet, the food and drink that the ships carried to feed the men was often poor. The salted meat, cheese, and biscuits quickly spoiled. Even the water and wine went bad. This left nothing on board fit for the men to eat or drink.

In the first stage of the voyage, Magellan led the ships to the Canary Islands off the northwestern coast of Africa. From there, the ships sailed across the Atlantic Ocean to South America.

Soon after they set sail, Magellan discovered that the Portuguese had bribed some of his officers to start a mutiny that would end the voyage. Magellan reacted quickly and put down the mutiny.

In December of 1519, Magellan and his ships reached Brazil. They sailed

into the bay where Rio de Janeiro is located today. This was Portuguese territory, but the Portuguese people living in Brazil were friendly. There, Magellan's sailors enjoyed their first taste of pineapples and the customs of the Brazilian people.

In December 1519, Magellan's fleet anchored off of what is now Rio de Janeiro, Brazil. There, natives greeted the sailors warmly. The Europeans spent most of the month basking in the beauty and friendliness of this paradise.

CLOSE-UP ON A SAILING SHIP

This ship is similar to the five ships that made up Magellan's fleet. His ships included (in order of size from largest to smallest) the *San Antonio*, the *Trinidad*, the *Victoria*, the *Concepción*, and the *Santiago*. Magellan offered the largest ship to one of his three Spanish captains while he piloted the *Trinidad*. This type of ship was approximately 70 feet (21 m) long. This would make the ship only slightly longer than a modern semitrailer, which averages about 65 feet (20 m) long. (See images at right for comparison.)

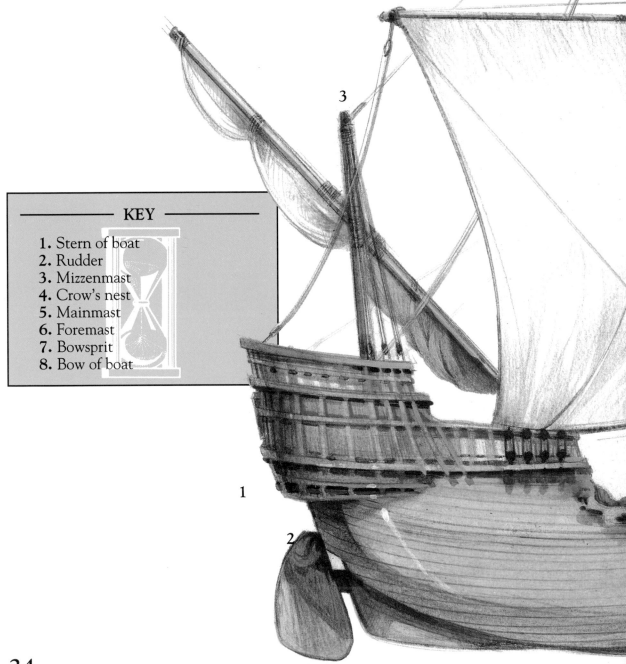

KEY

1. Stern of boat
2. Rudder
3. Mizzenmast
4. Crow's nest
5. Mainmast
6. Foremast
7. Bowsprit
8. Bow of boat

5

4

6

7

8

Magellan ordered his ships farther south. There, a storm forced them into a bay for protection. The sailors discovered that the bay was part of a greater waterway. Could this be the strait that passed through South America? Magellan ordered the crew to explore the bay at once. But the sailors were soon disappointed when they realized that the waterway was not a strait. Instead, it was merely another river. This river, which is now known as the Rio de la Plata, runs between Uruguay and Argentina.

The fleet journeyed still farther south. By February 1520, the ships approached the polar regions. There, the short Antarctic summer was almost over. As the coasts grew barren, the weather turned cold. Icy winds blasted the ships from the south, and fog blanketed the ocean.

The sailors were growing tired of it all. With little more than an hourglass and a compass to guide them, the men did their best. Still, they

Instruments such as the traverse board and the hourglass aided early explorers. The traverse board (above) was used to plot the ship's course, while the hourglass (top) measured time.

found no sign of any passageway through the continent. Also, although they had never liked their captain, who was Portuguese, they had put up with him. Now, however, Magellan was unbearable. He withstood the cold and the hardship. He pushed the fleet to sail farther and farther south.

Finally, at the end of March, Magellan led the ships into the bay of San Julian. There, the weary sailors rested, waiting for better weather. The fleet stayed five months. And from there, although no one knew it, the southern tip of South America was not far.

Penguins are abundant in the colder waters of the Southern Hemisphere. The Europeans had never before seen these "wingless ducks," as they called the birds.

PATAGONIAN PENGUIN.

On April 1, a mutiny broke out. The mutineers seized the *San Antonio*, the largest of the five ships. Two other ships, the *Concepción* and the *Victoria*, also turned against Magellan. Only the *Trinidad* and the *Santiago* remained loyal to their captain.

Again, Magellan reacted quickly. He had his loyal ships attack the *San Antonio*. Soon, all three disloyal ships were taken back under Magellan's control.

In August, the ships put to sea again and continued their route along the cold and barren shores of the land that came to be known as Patagonia. It was on these shores that the captain and his crew first saw seals and penguins.

Under cover of night, mutineers captured the *San Antonio* on April 1, 1520.

Magellan named the land Patagonia, which means "big foot," because of the size of the people who lived in the area. Magellan's crew reported seeing a race of giant people on shore. The sailors claimed these people stood over 7 feet (2 m) tall and wore no clothes despite the freezing weather.

At first meeting, the Europeans and the natives were friendly. But later, Magellan tried to capture two of the Patagonians to take back to Spain. The natives fought back and escaped, but in the struggle, one of Magellan's men was killed. Magellan feared that the natives would come back to harm his crew and ships. Despite the violent weather, he thought it best to move on.

As the expedition navigated its way into the lower end of the Santa Cruz River, the tiny *Santiago* became stranded on a sandbank. The crew leaped to safety, but the ship was destroyed by a powerful storm.

Winds of hurricane force pounded the other four ships as well. The winds broke the masts and tore sails. As the *San Antonio* and the *Concepción* were forced up onto the rocky shore of a bay, it looked as if the fate of these two ships would end in disaster as well.

But when the storm died down, all four remaining ships had survived. The storm had carried them past the rocks and into a channel that ran due west. No, this was not the entrance to just another lake or river. At last, on October 21, 1520, Magellan and his men realized they had found the passageway through South America.

As Magellan's fleet headed south along Patagonia, the sailors experienced the violent winds, called *pamperos*, for which the area is known. During one terrible storm, the *Santiago* was destroyed, and two other ships nearly met the same fate.

THE DREAM UNRAVELS

Standing in the stern of the longboat, Magellan navigates his fleet through rocky waters near the tip of South America.

Magellan's crew endured five weeks of cold, storm, and misery passing through the strait. Many of the men wanted to give up and go home to Spain. The crew of the mutineers' chief ship, the *San Antonio*, actually deserted. Under cover of night, the ship turned and made its way back to Spain.

Magellan, firm as always, would not turn back. Despite the horrid conditions, he drove his remaining three ships onward. The ships finally passed through the strait and into the second ocean on November 28, 1520. At the sight of the ocean that he named the Pacific, tears of happiness rolled down Magellan's face.

The next part of the voyage meant crossing

the Pacific Ocean to reach Asia. Magellan and his crew had been at sea for fourteen months. One ship had been wrecked. Another had deserted. The remaining three were short on food, but the men were not worried. They were certain that islands along the way would offer fresh supplies. Sadly, they were wrong.

The ships traveled mile after mile, and no islands came into view. Day after day, week after week, and month after month, the ships sailed on into the Pacific, surrounded by an endless expanse of sea.

With great joy, Ferdinand Magellan views the Pacific Ocean for the first time in November 1520.

A map of the world shows the details of Magellan's journey. Although no one knew for certain that a ship could sail from the Atlantic Ocean to the Pacific Ocean, many believed that this was possible. Magellan was intent on proving it.

On the map: The part of the journey sailed under Magellan's command is indicated in pink. The part of the journey that was completed after Magellan's death is shown in green.

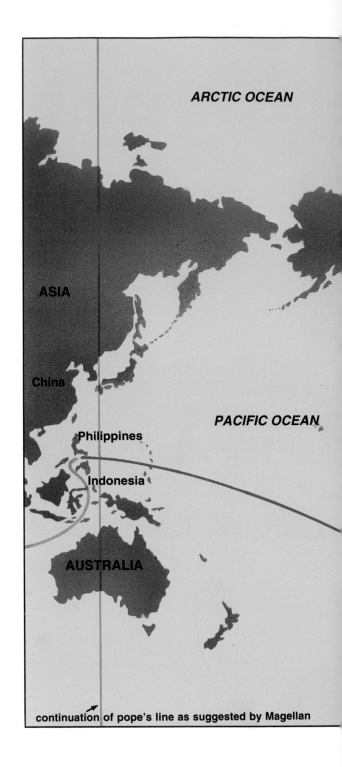

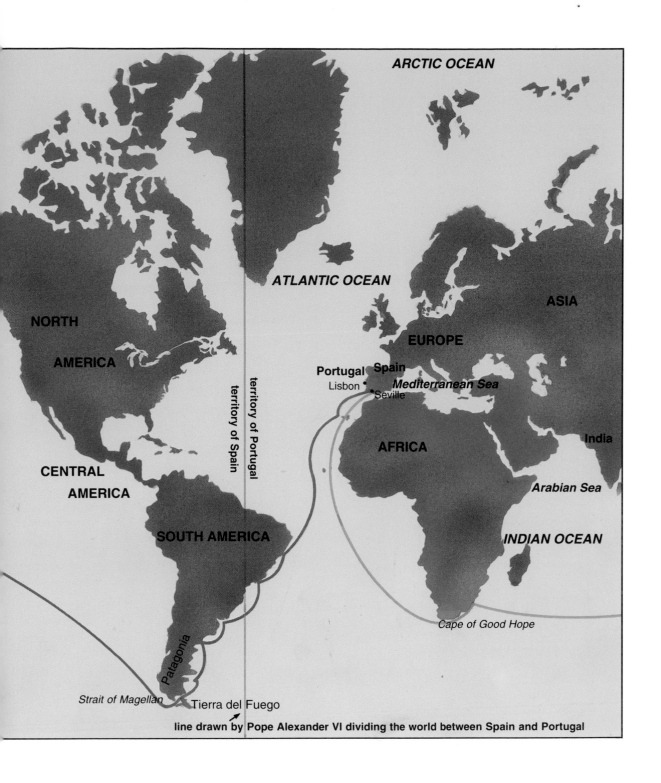

ARCTIC OCEAN

ATLANTIC OCEAN

ASIA

NORTH

AMERICA

EUROPE

Portugal   Spain

Lisbon •
•Seville

Mediterranean Sea

territory of Portugal

territory of Spain

India

AFRICA

Arabian Sea

CENTRAL

AMERICA

SOUTH AMERICA

INDIAN OCEAN

Patagonia

Cape of Good Hope

Strait of Magellan   Tierra del Fuego

line drawn by Pope Alexander VI dividing the world between Spain and Portugal

As their food supplies dwindled, Magellan's men became desperate. What biscuits they still had were full of insects, but they ate them anyway. They caught rats aboard the ships and ate them. The men even ate sawdust and leather. Nineteen men died of scurvy, a disease caused by a lack of vitamin C that is found in fruits and vegetables. It was a wonder that anyone survived at all.

On March 7, 1521, Magellan and his crew finally came upon an island known today as Guam. When the people of the island stole the small skiff that had carried Magellan's men to shore, Magellan attacked the natives. In his fury, he killed a number of them.

After that, Magellan's men quickly stocked up on fresh food and water. Once they had loaded their boats with all the vegetables, bananas, coconuts, fish, and pigs they could carry, they were ready to sail westward again.

On March 16, Magellan reached the islands that were later named the Philippines in honor of King Philip II of Spain. The people of these islands greeted Magellan and his men warmly. Claiming the islands for Spain, Magellan then began converting the people to Christianity.

Magellan's men suffered for weeks without proper food or fresh water. Had Magellan chosen a route just slightly to the south, he would have encountered many islands.

Magellan continued to explore other nearby islands. He wanted to claim them all for Spain and convert the people to Christianity. It was religion now — more than adventure or commerce — that drove Magellan.

On the island of Cebu, Magellan again found friendly natives. He converted many of them, including their leader, Sultan Humabon. Then, to prove his friendship, Magellan offered to attack Humabon's enemy on the neighboring island of Mactan.

When Magellan and his men landed on Mactan on April 27, 1521, over one thousand islanders were waiting, prepared to fight. Although Magellan had only sixty men with him, he

ordered the attack anyway. With guns and armor, he was confident that they could win.

But weapons were not enough to help Magellan in his bungled attack. The islanders quickly drove the invaders back toward their ships. Magellan, covering his retreating men, was killed. He would never complete the voyage he had begun.

With only a small band of volunteers, Magellan attacked the people of Mactan, an island in the Philippines. Coming ashore, the Europeans were surprised to find over one thousand natives waiting for them. The battle cost Magellan his life.

6

COMPLETING THE CIRCLE

Now in a state of disarray, what was left of Magellan's fleet set sail once again. Fortunately, the sailors were now in familiar waters. From Portuguese accounts, they knew where the Indonesian islands were located and how to get home from there.

When the ships reached the islands in November 1521, the natives welcomed them. The sailors, weary from their travels, stayed for nearly three months.

In February 1522, the ships sailed again. Loaded with spices, the ships left the islands

The voyage became even more chaotic after Magellan's death. In separate incidents, the *Concepción* was burned (below), and the *Trinidad* sank (opposite).

and sailed westward across the Indian Ocean. When they reached the eastern coast of Africa, they found the area dominated by the Portuguese. They did not dare land.

On May 6, 1522, they passed the Cape of Good Hope at Africa's southern tip. By now, only one ship, the *Victoria*, remained, and it was leaking. Earlier, the sailors had burned the *Concepción*, because they no longer had enough men to sail three ships. Then the *Trinidad* sank because the men had overloaded it with spices. Juan Sebastian del Cano, who had been one of the mutineers two years earlier, led the *Victoria* and the remaining sailors.

On September 8, 1522, the *Victoria* finally returned home to Spain. The voyage to the Far East had been a costly one, taking over three years and many men's lives to complete. A total of about 270 men and five ships had set sail with Magellan on September 20, 1519. Only one ship and 18 of those men came home.

Still, Magellan's voyage had been a success. He had found the passage to the second ocean, and his ships had sailed beyond that ocean to the Far East. But the greater success of Magellan's voyage was the journey itself. The *Victoria* had sailed completely around the earth. No ship had done that before.

After over three years at sea, a sick, weary, and worn band of sailors dragged themselves into the church of Santa Maria de la Victoria in Seville.

THE LEGACY OF MAGELLAN

Ferdinand Magellan's name is linked forever with that of the ocean he named, the Pacific. Today, Magellan is honored as one of the world's greatest navigators and explorers. The strait that he discovered, now known as the Strait of Magellan, marks that honor. In Magellan's day, the strait was an important find. Its discovery meant that ships could sail freely from the Atlantic Ocean to the Pacific Ocean and back. This freedom offered endless trade possibilities to the European exploring nations.

But in time, Magellan's work proved far more important than even this. His voyage had proved beyond a doubt that the earth was a sphere. It also showed that this sphere was covered with one great stretch of ocean. The continents, people now knew, were like huge islands set in that ocean.

Magellan, of course, did not live long enough to complete the voyage himself. But his foresight and his sense of adventure were greatly responsible for its completion. Through that voyage, the entire world was opened to navigation. That, more than anything, may have been Ferdinand Magellan's greatest contribution to history.

CHRONOLOGY

1480 Ferdinand Magellan is born in Portugal.

1487 Bartholomew Dias, a Portuguese navigator, reaches the southern tip of Africa.

1492 Italian navigator Christopher Columbus claims the American continents for Spain.

1493 Pope Alexander VI draws an imaginary line through the Atlantic Ocean, dividing all newly "discovered" territories between Spain and Portugal.

Ferdinand Magellan becomes a page in the court of King John II and Queen Leonor of Portugal.

1495 King John II dies. Duke Manuel succeeds him as king of Portugal.

1497 Portuguese navigator Vasco da Gama sails around Africa and reaches India.

1505 Magellan enlists as a sailor and sails with a Portuguese fleet to the Far East.

1511- Magellan, now an officer, returns
1512 to Portugal. As part of the Portuguese army, he goes to Morocco, where Portugal is fighting for control. There he is rumored to be selling captured livestock for his own gain.

1513 Spanish explorer Vasco Núñez de Balboa enters Panama and sights the "South Sea" that is now known as the Pacific Ocean. Magellan believes that this might be a second ocean, and that if ships sail far enough west on it, they can reach the Far East.

1514- Magellan returns to Portugal.
1516 Having lost favor with King Manuel, he is discharged.

1517 Magellan leaves Portugal forever. He travels to Spain.

1518 Magellan convinces King Charles I of Spain to sponsor his search for a new route to the Far East through the Americas.

1519 **September 20** — With five ships and about 270 men, Magellan sets sail for the Far East.

1520 **October 21** — Magellan finds the passageway, or strait, through the Americas. Passing through the strait, Magellan loses two ships. **November 28** — The fleet reaches the second ocean, which Magellan names the Pacific.

1521 The ships reach islands now known as the Mariana Islands and the Philippines. **April 27** — Magellan is killed on the island of Mactan.

1522 **September 8** — The *Victoria* returns to Spain.

GLOSSARY

bribe: Money or other valuables offered to someone to try to win that person's favor or influence his or her decisions.

channel: A body of water that connects two larger bodies of water. The English Channel, for example, connects the Atlantic Ocean and the North Sea.

circumnavigate: To go all the way around something, especially by water. Magellan was the first to circumnavigate the world.

convert: To convince a person to change from one belief, view, or idea to another. Many early explorers and missionaries tried to convert native peoples from their customary religious beliefs to Christianity.

empire: A group of lands or nations that is ruled by a single ruler or government.

Far East: The name given to the countries of eastern Asia. Europeans wanted to trade with the Far East for products unavailable in Europe.

isthmus: A strip of land that connects two larger areas of land.

mutiny: An open rebellion against authority by soldiers, sailors, or other subordinates. In a mutiny, rebels known as mutineers refuse to obey orders and may attempt to overthrow their leader.

navigator: The crew member of a ship or aircraft who plots the course that is to be followed.

nobility: A class of people born to high social status and, usually, wealth. In Europe during Magellan's time, generally only people of nobility were educated. This, in part, accounts for why there were no commoners among the first explorers.

page: A young person, usually a boy, being trained as a knight or learning to serve a knight or other person of nobility.

patriotism: A feeling of great love for and loyalty to one's country. Patriotism led many early sailors to explore and conquer new lands for their countries.

pension: A sum of money regularly paid to a person, often after he or she has retired from work because of age or disability.

scurvy: A disease resulting from a lack of vitamin C, marked by bleeding gums and loose teeth. Many sailors on early voyages of exploration suffered from scurvy because they went for long periods of time without foods, such as vegetables and fresh fruit, that supply the body with vitamin C.

sphere: A three-dimensional object that is shaped in such a way that all of the points on its surface are the same distance from the center point. The earth and the other planets are spheres. Before the voyages of exploration, many Europeans thought that the earth was flat.

strait: A narrow passage of water that connects two larger bodies of water (*see* **channel**).

MORE TO READ

The following reading materials will tell you more about Ferdinand Magellan, his times, and the places he explored, as well as other great explorers.

Explorers and Discovery. Cass R. Sandak (Franklin Watts)

Ferdinand Magellan, Noble Captain. Katherine Wilke (Houghton Mifflin)

The First Ships Around the World. Walter Brownlee (Lerner)

Great Adventures That Changed Our World. (Reader's Digest Association)

The Great Explorers. Piers Pennington (Facts on File)

Great Lives: Exploration. Milton Lomask (Macmillan)

Who Really Discovered America? Stephen Krensky (Scholastic)

The Discovery of America: Opposing Viewpoints. Renardo Barden (Greenhaven)

PLACES TO WRITE

The following organizations can give you more information about Ferdinand Magellan and his legacy. When you write, always be specific in your questions. Be sure to include your full name, age, return address, and a return envelope for a reply.

National Maritime Historical Society
P.O. Box 646
Croton-on-Hudson, New York 15020

South American Explorer's Club
P.O. Box 18327
Denver, Colorado 80218

American Geographical Society Collection
Golda Meir Library
University of Wisconsin-Milwaukee
P.O. Box 604
Milwaukee, Wisconsin 53201

OTHER ACTIVITIES

1. Do any European explorers figure in the history of the area where you live? Find traces of these explorers in the names of cities, towns, rivers, or other geographical features; in the religion and culture of the area; or in the people themselves.

2. What is the other side of the story concerning the European "discovery" of the Americas? How did the arrival of the Europeans affect the American Indian tribes who may have lived where you now live?

3. Several people have recently made attempts to circumnavigate the earth in sailboats. Find out about these people. Were their voyages successful? How long did they take to circle the world? What hardships did they face along the way?

INDEX